A Clown at Midnight

Books by Andrew Hudgins

A Clown at Midnight

ANDREW HUDGINS

A MARINER ORIGINAL

Mariner Books

Houghton Mifflin Harcourt

Boston   New York

2013

Copyright © 2013 by Andrew Hudgins

For information about permission to reproduce selections from this book,
write to Permissions, Houghton Mifflin Harcourt Publishing Company,
215 Park Avenue South, New York, New York 10003.

www.hmhbooks.com

Library of Congress Cataloging-in-Publication Data
Hudgins, Andrew.
[Poems. Selections]
A clown at midnight / Andrew Hudgins.
pages cm
ISBN 978-0-544-10880-6
1. Title.
PS3558.U288C56 2013
811'.54—dc23
2013000391

Book design by Greta D. Sibley

Printed in the United States of America

DOC 10 9 8 7 6 5 4 3 2 1

Contents

3

4

Agathon arose in order that he might take his place on the couch by Socrates, when suddenly a band of revellers entered, and spoiled the order of the banquet. Someone who was going out having left the door open, they had found their way in, and made themselves at home; great confusion ensued, and everyone was compelled to drink large quantities of wine. Aristodemus said . . . he was awakened towards daybreak by a crowing of cocks, and . . . there remained only Socrates, Aristophanes, and Agathon, who were drinking out of a large goblet which they passed round, and Socrates was discoursing to them. Aristodemus was only half awake, and he did not hear the beginning of the discourse; the chief thing which he remembered was Socrates compelling the other two to acknowledge that the genius of comedy was the same with that of tragedy, and that the true artist in tragedy was an artist in comedy also. To this they were constrained to assent, being drowsy, and not quite following the argument.

—Plato, *Symposium* (translated by Benjamin Jowett)

I

A Joke Is Washed Up on a Desert Island

A joke is washed up on an island,
miles of coarse, brown grit
and a few bent palms. He's thrilled. Alone,
he'll stroll the beach or sit

mulling the gray surf and his life.
He believes he's kept the sacred
sacred by profaning it.
But words and stories sped

so quickly from his raucous mouth
he hardly thought about them.
Alone, he'll study doubts he's had
since on a dubious whim

he swaggered into that first brothel,
first bar and first bar mitzvah,
first monastery. What angry hope
or compulsive mania

flung him on the judgment of friends
and strangers: a laugh or silence?
He'd never paused to mull things over,
and though thinking's a nuisance,

it's time to think. He sits, considers,
and the teasing sea deposits

a naked beauty at his feet—
a movie star. Huge tits?

Or small? Full lips or thin? You choose.
Whatever turns your crank,
that's what floats up. And then two more,
beautiful, blond, and blank.

They swirl around him, asking, "Is *that*
a banana in your pocket?"
Smart women whoring for a joke!
And all at once he gets it:

the human cost of laughter. It pains him.
The people he's offended,
they're human, unlike him, a concept
he'd never comprehended—

a reverie of thick self-pity
that's broken by a shout
of "Help me! Help me!" from the waves.
Annoyed, the joke swims out

and finds an armless, legless man
bobbing in the spray.
"I'm Bob. Remember me?" Bob shouts.
The joke saves him anyway.

The joke has always hated Bob,
the lamest slip of wit,
and now Bob's propped on the joke's beach,
choking and spraying spit.

The joke stares down the empty sand,
listening hopelessly
for the peace he'd hoped to find. He drags
Bob back into the sea.

At first Bob bobs, but head held under,
he blubbers, bubbles, drowns.
This joke's a killer. He looks out to sea,
sees what he sees, and frowns.

The waves are pitching with old punch lines,
washing, like Natalie Wood,
ashore. They couldn't live without him,
although he'd hoped they could.

As each one staggers from the waves,
it asks, "Where's Bob?" The joke
says, "He'll turn up." Why are they asking?
Who cares about that jerk?

He's got to blow this island, man.
He jumps into the sea.

But he's my joke. I send a shark
and the shark chomps off one knee.

He keeps on kicking at the waves.
The shark chomps off both legs.
"Very funny!" screams the joke. "So now
I'm Bob. Come on," he begs.

"Let me be Art!" Tear out this page
and pin it to your wall:
He's Art. Or throw it on the floor.
Bingo, he's Matt. Your call.

But I like the turning point of jokes.
He'll bob, but he won't sink.
Let's leave him there to meditate.
The shark will help him think.

Three pale blonds gather on the beach
to watch him flail. In moonlight
their roots turn dark, their hair turns black.
Their eyes are old-moon white.

Birth of a Naturalist

Among moist bromeliads
I was bored, and the soft-fingered
ferns annoyed me like an aunt
touching my face and trailing
her fingers down my cheek.
What was I, a possession?
In the gift shop where I desired
nothing, a stranger confused
boredom for balked desire
and bought me a small pot
with a blunt nub, like a toad's
brown snout, jutting
from dry soil. "Thank you," I said.
"Thank you," as I'd been taught,
and she departed, a plump whorl
of black hair and red scarves.
In my pocket, the pot rode
my thigh like a damp stone,
and because it was a secret,
my secret, I began to love it.
The next day the toad's
tumescent snout, now mossy green,
cracked the packed dirt.
On the windowsill a rickety stalk
rose and kept rising, rising
until it fell into my bed,
and with the toppled orchid in my arms,

I slept until Mother's laughter
woke me, and I was shamed.
Again in secret, I tucked
its roots in spongy humus
beyond our lawn, where, spindly
and limp-leafed, it dwindled.
Now when I stretch out
over its absence, the coarse
vigor of its killers cushions me,
and I see the lost
orchid animating bracken,
buckthorn, buttercup, and bramble.
Morning glory overclimbs it all,
green on green, blaring
its beautiful and murderous
alabaster trumpets
while twizzling vines unfurl,
spin in sunlight, and, clutching,
caress my face.

First Year out of School

A man . . . may have wild birds in an aviary; these in one
sense he possesses, and in another he has none of them.

—Plato, *Theaetetus*

I fingered flannel shirts
and wrinkled seed potatoes,
derelict in dusty bins,
but bought a birdcage,
white paint peeling off
corroded wire. For weeks
it crowded my bedside table
until, walking to work,
I heard baby rabbits
mewing in a hole. Later,
at my desk, I watched a crow
ferry three gray lumps
to an oak limb and pick them
into red strings. In one
imagined life, I caught
that crow and taught it Blake—
Little Lamb, who made thee?
In another, I gleaned raw corn
from nearby fields at night,
fed it to the strident crow,
and every night after work
cleaned its fetid cage.

In this life, I sold the cage
for a quarter what I paid,
and moved to a city where,
on the street one Monday morning,
a man chanted, "Spare
change, spare change,
spare change," so rote
that like everyone before me
I didn't bother saying no.
I was no different. Why then
did he block my path
and offer me a matted,
damp, dark thing—
a hatchling half held,
half nestled in his beard?
And why did I linger over
the unfledgeable lump?
"No," I said, pushing past,
but after an hour I returned
and with five grubby ones
paid for the epiphany
he'd led me to: I yearn for flight,
but believe in the two
reliable slow feet
on which I stood, receiving
from his hands unto mine
a gasping, unsalvable mouth.

A Clown at Midnight

The essence of true horror is a clown at midnight.
—Lon Chaney Sr.

Down these mean streets a bad joke walks alone,
bruised head held low, chin tucked in tight, eyes down,
defiant. He laughs and it turns to a moan.

His wife left years ago, and his kids all groan,
claim they have never heard of him, and frown.
Down these mean streets a bad joke walks alone,

jiving with fat whores in the combat zone
and moving on each time they put him down.
Defiant, he laughs though it turns to a moan—

a sense of humor turning on its own
sick pivot. He knows you think he's just a clown.
Down these mean streets a bad joke walks alone.

He *is* a clown—but dangerous, flyblown,
stinking of the bitterest cologne.
Defiant, he laughs and it turns to a moan.

He doesn't want to rub your funny bone.
He wants to break it—break it, then skip town.
Down these mean streets a bad joke walks alone
but defiant. He laughs and it turns to a moan.

In the Arboretum

As a lowering snowstorm
silk-screened the arboretum
into a gauzy tomb
around an ecosystem
stalled summer in late autumn,
I slid along the stem
of a tropical leaf a thumb
still frigid, slow to accustom
myself to the steam
drifting like a phantom
through the rich spectrum
of greenery, each item
doomed outside the sanctum.
Inside: one desideratum.
Outside, let's imagine: time
and the obscuring storm.
In a breath or two I'll join them,
fingering a green stem,
a pinched and withering victim
that is, a card states, false thyme.

I Saw My Shadow Walking

I saw my shadow walking south
on Market Street at dawn.
He had a long gun in his hand,
a Winchester 1901.

He held it in the air and waved.
I wondered if I'd died.
He walked down to the children's park
and sat down on the slide.

I hadn't seen him for two weeks.
He'd slipped his medication
and stolen from beneath my bed
my Winchester 1901.

The cops told him to drop the gun.
He squinted at the sun
as he swung up and aimed at them
that Winchester 1901.

Grace Pittman opened her front door
and bent to fetch the news
when she heard two pistol shots resound
as she said in interviews.

"I looked and saw the shadow drop
like a punctured bag of air,"

Grace Pittman told reporters,
who didn't really care.

My shadow wasn't dangerous.
The point, I guess, is moot.
He must have hated me so much
he forced the cops to shoot.

I scrubbed his blood off slide and swings,
and shadowless in sun,
I walked to city hall and claimed
my Winchester 1901.

In Arcadia, the Home of Pan

You mock us acorn scroungers.
"How the bitter nut shrivels their lips!"
you say—you eaters of milled grain,
  you who've never seen

even the raw dough, even
the hot loaves shoveled from the oven.
You tear them and devour them,
  your soft bread alien,

arriving with the dew.
Mock us who harvest bitter nuts,
who pound them, soak them, grind them, chew
  rough, crumbling acorn bread.

Mock us—you mock our god,
the goat god. Mock him. Have your fun.
Pass by his shrines. Neglect old gods
  with secret names, and soon

your hogs fail even in cool weather,
your horses pull up lame, crops wither,
the hunter stumbles, women keen
  as daughters bleed obscenely.

Soon your woven robes
rot and fall from your white shoulders.

You eaters of honeyed oat cakes soon
   haunt the dark woods, and moan

  for acorns and twisted lips.
Go tell the god storms sank your ships,
your oil jar's dry, your manhood drips.
  Tell him your brilliant quips.

  He might reward your wit
with bitter flour flecked with grit
from shattered acorn shells. Admit
  your soft souls hunger for it.

Steppingstone

Home (*from Court Square Fountain —*
where affluent ghosts still importune
a taciturn
slave to entertain
them with a slow barbarous tune
in his auctioned baritone —
to Hank Williams's headstone
atop a skeleton
loose in a pristine
white suit and bearing a pristine
white Bible, to the black bloodstain
on Martin King's torn
white shirt and Jim Clark's baton,
which smashed black skulls to gelatin)
was home, at fifteen: brimstone
on Sunday morning, badminton
hot afternoons, and brimstone
again that night. Often,
as the preacher flailed the lectern,
the free grace I couldn't sustain
past lunch led to clandestine
speculation. Skeleton
and flesh, bone and protein
hold — or is it detain? —
my soul. Was my hometown
Montgomery's molten
sunlight or the internal nocturne

of my unformed soul? Was I torn
from time or was time torn
from me? Turn
on byzantine
turn, I entertain
possibilities still, and overturn
most. It's routine
now to call a hometown
a steppingstone—
and a greased, uncertain,
aleatory stone
at that. Metaphors attune
our ears to steppingstone,
as well as corner-, grind-, and millstone—
all obtain
and all also cartoon
history, which like a piston,
struck hard and often
that blood-dappled town
scrubbed with the acetone
of American inattention. Atone
me no atoning. We know the tune,
and as we sing it we attain
a slow, wanton,
and puritan
grace, grace can't contain.

The Offices

Whether we have slept
through Matins' dream offices
or lain awake, we rise
to a morning bell we do not
call Lauds, and not calling it
ablution, we, for the day's
offices, flush dust
and dead skin from our many
creases. On the highway
and at computers pinging all day
with the needs and even dreams
of those to whom we minister,
we labor at gratitude through long
and exhausting offices
we do not call Terces, Sexts,
and Nones. At Vespers we share
with our bodies a meal not
exactly a Eucharist,
and before the Compline bell's
imagined ringing, we
indulge in bourbon, sex,
or prayer, and then lie down,
thankful for tomorrow's impossible
offices, apostles prospering
somehow under the Lord's
preposterous auspices.

Autumn's Author

In his dissolving mansion, autumn's author
is an exhausted autocrat, dying faster
than the falling house is falling. Rainfall, raw
and raucous, claws the roof as he dodders down
broad halls, rattling knobs inalterably locked.
Once all gloss, paunch, and wanton frivolity,
he's now all thought, not somersault or song,
and he wonders what those lost enthrallments meant.
He knows they weren't false, though behind the last,
unlocked knob, a chalk-faced pallbearer coughs.

2

Shall I laugh with Democritus, or weep with Heraclitus?

—Robert Burton, *The Anatomy of Melancholy*

At Evening, Eden

At evening, Eden
—under grenadine
skies that harden
and glow till dawn—
quiets. The din
of birdsong thins down
to one bird's one
trembling tendon,
and under a linden
man and maiden
vow love's condign
vows—now mundane,
then new, golden,
and yet undone.
You're God. Condone
their pure abandon.
Kiss, hug, disdain
—all firsts—embolden
the distant dawn.
More vows and abandon,
tainted now—
she bites his hand on
the palm, hard, done
to pin down
faith incarnadine.

You're still God. Ordain
the murderous dawn
as it brightens. Adorn
their days with red dawn
and red sundown—
like blood, but iodine.

Mattress under Sumac

Heavy with the day
and a failed hunt, I lay
down on a mattress dumped
beneath sumac. Rifle
cradled in my arms, I slept
on the mattress everyone
joked about, saying they
had never used it, but
one boy claimed Caroline
Aldridge had stumbled out
of red, autumn sumac,
hanging on a stranger,
her shoes hooked on his fingers,
and after that I was driven
with doubt, disgust, and newly
hopeful desire, knowing
the many ways I'd loved her,
tenderly or forceful
while alone, and the mattress
served my mastering
imagination for years,
before, in the mesmerizing
musk of autumn sumac,
I, one morning, woke.

Swordfish

My fingertips marveled at the silvery shimmer,
already less silver, less shimmery than when it lived.
I never again should cause flesh this beautiful
to be less beautiful, I thought.
                                        At supper
—swordfish—my brother offered up his neighbor
for conversation. He'd shotgunned every TV
in his house, even the puny black-and-white
on the kitchen counter. Buckshot shattered black
granite and splintered yards of golden oak.

In the unexpected hush as we considered
slaughtered appliances, my brother's drinking buddy
told my girlfriend she was a pretty lady,
a real pretty lady. She looked like a dream.
One day she'd make a real man really happy.
I barked three hard flat laughs. The lit friend winced
as each blast turned his cheeks a richer red.
My girlfriend closed her eyes and opened them,
her azure eyelids shimmering with jade.

Fairy Tale with Ex-Wife

After thirty suspect miles, I stood in flurries,
a rusty PURE sign creaking overhead,
and called. We were right: we were wrong.
The storm we were trying to beat, beat down on us,
and by the time we slid, white-faced, up
the gravel drive, ice-bright trees burned
with horizontal light.

                Out here,
the TV couldn't get a signal, the old
woman croaked, but it worked fine, fine,
and we could always bring it back. All night
we huddled on her living room's gold shag
and shivered. At eight, she handed us a pot
of watery lentils, spiked with tiny twigs,
maybe rosemary, and a single black plum.
"Hansel," you said. "Gretel," I chuckled, moving
my hand along the front seam of your jeans
till, arching back, you tensed, and then subsided
against my chest. When I put your hand on me,
you said, "She'll catch us." Then: "Goddamn it, no."

I woke in blue ice-light and reached for the plum.
You'd nipped it. I bit it open at the wound
and sucked the bursting juice, the yellow flesh
like sunlight glistening through the torn black skin

down to the wet stone, which I pocketed.
At dawn, we skittered to the interstate,
and in a Waffle House we drank till noon
from what the waitress called a bottomless cup
while giant trucks scraped clear the highway home.

Star Jasmine

Starless star jasmine
swarmed the gnomon,
sprawled on the mown
grass under the moon
and three stars. A moan,
low, answered mine,
and moon-blue semen
starred her moon-
white abdomen.
My heart was mean.
I could not determine
half denouement
from all amen.
Beside star jasmine
I saw no stamen
furred with pollen,
but a common
and heavy sermon
pervaded the domain:
the scent of woman
and man. Ambrosial jasmine
claimed the gnomon
and the man and woman.
It yearned for the moon,
even for the amen,
but there'd been no amen.
I was wrong, I mean.
There had been no sermon.

Laid Off

After I'd been laid off,
my boss's boss
called. Her urgency
almost unmanned me.
She took pleasure
like conjuring a trance
that resisted unbelievers.
Poor locked body—how
could I stop her thinking?
As she finished, I
swam through a warm
and sybaritic sea
to a green island
blurred on the horizon
and then, briefly, stark
against moonrise. She
was a beauty, the beauty
eroding softly around
bronze eyes and decisive mouth.
That month I didn't
wear shoes, and when
she told me it was time
to move on, I stuttered:
Buh, buh, buh, bulging
with effort to mount
that citadel with just
my lips: *Born*, it came out,

electrifying us both—once
in twenty-seven times.
You've done that,
haven't you? Counted?
It's the spoon with which
I eat the moon, spooning
one curved scoop
of blue melon, savoring
it until it's savorless,
then spooning another
slice of beautiful moon,
when, in June, it rhymes.

At the DMV

At the DMV, I'd already
assessed the ass,
compact beneath taut
blue charmeuse,
of a woman in line, and
I was staring nowhere,
thinking nothing,
when she walked past
and without stopping said,
"White shirt, khaki pants.
You haven't changed."
Two nights later, as I slid
toward another dream
of water-damaged houses,
marred love, and tense
friendships, the shape of her name
like virga between my face
and a hunter's moon
—almost Brenda or Linda,
almost McSomething—
nearly came back to me.

Princess after Princess

Pink eggs tucked into pinker baskets, they changed
to princesses again, surpassing now
a reverie of Easter, their satin and sateen
belilaced, enrosed, and daisied among the yellow,
resurrected dandelions.
                              "Me next!
Me next!" they ordered, as on my knee I bounced
each beauty, beating hoofbeats on my thighs
and assuring one, two, and three they were beautiful,
until I boosted the fourth onto the tiring legs
of Uncle Horse. Gobbets of chocolate
blotted her chin and cotton violets.
Ire stiffened her overbite, and I was slow to lie.
"You didn't say I was beautiful!" she blurted.
The thunderbolt face of a sunburnt mother turned.
"*Of course* you're beautiful!"

                              "Tell me again!"
The frantic horse began to gallop. "You're beautiful."
"Again!"
            "Bee-yoo-tee-ful," I sang.
                                          "Again."
Lie, liar, and the undeceived—
hoofbeats, feigned hoofbeats, carried us away.

In the Lounge

To a hotel
lounge's pastel
near-jazz, my barstool
swivels over Carrara tile
and beneath a crystal
girandole. To the tall
lovely beside her, the tall
lovely beside me waxes anecdotal
about her marital
malaises, stale
in every detail—
him, her: coital
inexclusivity. A horsetail
fern tickles my neck and its gentle
fronds screen my incidental
eavesdropping till,
bored, I order another cocktail
and steel
my nerves against two volatile
Scotch-and-rocks, who extol
their mental
superiority to every wastrel
here in the state capital,
every one a congenital
and monumental
fuck-up. Avid, wary, almost hostile,

they survey the clientele,
and their gazes settle
on my appraised and still
appraising femme fatales
in the making. The men curtail
indecision, and stand. One's barstool
squeaks. One smooths his shirttail,
and at that pivotal
instant, they stall
as if they can foretell
all four lives' subtle,
or perhaps mortal,
altering. Bills swish into the till
and silver scratches out the elemental
jazz of retail,
metal
brushes stroking tuned metal
on the hi-hat. But no, nothing subtle
survives the lost contrapuntal
moment. "What you call that hairstyle?
It's gorgeous." I settle
back and tap my glass, another cocktail
imminent. The myrtle
trembles in the green bud: the lovelies necessarily fatale,
the men merely fatal.
The music's catchy, quick, and noncommittal.

There, There

Bent over the roaring cradle,
I felt like a crocodile
as, in the dark puddle
of my shadow, the beloved bundle
yodeled terror. I leaned
closer, mugging, and failed
to wheedle
a smile or even a lull
from the rage-ruddled
face. He bellowed
until his mother cuddled
him into her neck (blond
sweep of hair, cologne), and he lolled
in indolent *oohs* and coddling
there-theres. The ululations dwindled
into gurgles and drool.
His diaper yellowed.
She offered him to me. Barelegged,
he hung between us, his feet pedaling
fetid air until she lodged
him in my hands. He smelled
of Italian irises and lime—her cologne—
as did I. Astraddle
my hip, enclosed

in her perfume, he blabbed
happily while I dandled
him—*there, there*—loved
in the constricting middle.

Visiting an Old Love

"I'm sorry to hear your mother is unwell."
A bowl of decomposing roses, buds still closed,
sat on a glass shelf on a mirrored wall,
doubled against an image from outside:
sun-bleached autumn stubble, gray with rain.
Stop it, I told my eyes. But they could not.
"We argued till I knew we'd fall in love,"
you said, "and then we kept on arguing."
"No, we didn't," I said, laughed, and waited
for laughter. Or an argument. Or both.
"The shorter, darker days slip by unnoticed,
Mother says." I replied, "But you, you're well?"
"The rain might turn to wet snow any minute."
Eyes don't stop and neither does the weather.

Under the Maypole

Ribbons, pearl and purple,
dangle from the maypole
down to the pale
hands of children, who pull
them, giggling. They purl
in breezes and almost rumple.
Under the old eyes of a principal
whose narrow glance is ample
to subdue but not appall,
the children spill
around the skinned and limbless maple.
Bells peal.
Old tunes impose their spell
on the awkward small feet they impel
around the resurrection pole.
The pattern's simple,
plaiting boy to pearl
and girl to purple,
and when their fingers touch the pole
and the ribbons, at last, rumple,
no lips purse, no faces crumple
except one teacher's, and I can't spoil
the day's innocent and un-innocent appeal,
which terminates April's
cold intermittent pall.

Love Poem

It's an alliance,
the white pine
sending up
positive leaders
and the negative leaders
forking downward
from cumulonimbus
darkness, till
jittering opposites
touch, and the black
cloud discharges
down the passage
and into our pine
a Zeusian godfuck.
Lit for an instant
we didn't see
—not elegance,
but light, fire,
and shattering—
the front yard pine
tilted onto an oak.
Arriving home,
we paused, warm
in unexpected
sunlight, mystified.

Above us, a new
portal of bottomless
azure opened,
and in the soft light
we marveled first
at how we'd changed.

Foresworn

Not twenty now or twelve,
no girl-child remembers pink
plush monsters awaiting her
as she harnessed sensibility.
She can neither fondly conflate
the sun-starved and sunlit
houses in which I raised her
nor remember spinning inches
from blazing candelabra
we never owned, secure
in my uncertain hands,
nor will she remember
those hands cracking her quick
insolent lips or the chastened,
evasive days and decades
I watch the morning trees
dim into evening and darken
into midnight trees. With two wives
I have foresworn thee, daughter,
and your thrilling materiality
in the flesh's rage. In me
no father pines for your
embodiment, and my true daughter's
too composed to cry out
for incarnation and its cares.

The Wild Swans Skip Coole

We beat wings,
fly rings. We

scorn Yeats. We
have mates. We

won't stay. We
fly 'way.

3

A Mystery

Returning the polished silver to its place,
Trudy discovered the Master's body sprawled
across the Persian rug, exactly as,
three months before, she'd been appalled

to find the Mistress dead in the Queen Anne chair.
Inspector Smythe suspected Trudy first.
Though Trudy despised the murdered pair
because they never let her have a moment's rest

and always fussed about her sloppy work,
she had the palsy in her wrists and fingers both
and couldn't have snapped their thin patrician necks
in such a gruesome manner. Her husband, Booth,

could rip the caps off bottled beer barehanded
and sometimes—on a bet—he'd use his teeth.
But for the times his employers turned up dead
his alibis were ironclad, and Smythe

could never prove he wasn't at the pub
tossing back stout and swapping smutty stories
at the monthly meeting of the Butlers' Club.
Searching their rooms, Smythe found some BVDs

in Trudy's closet, skirts and hose in Booth's.
The two ex-actors had exchanged their parts
so they could kill and still confound the sleuths.
But Smythe saw through their cunning art.

Reality, he said, was not the same as show:
"Trudy is Booth, Booth Trudy—that is all we needed to know."

The Humor Institute

Officials at the Humor Institute
are sick of your crank calls. Would you please page
Anita Dick and Fonda Peters? No.

We'll help plan suitable retirement dinners—
no morbid jokes and no unseemly glee.
We'll help you lighten up the office when

a senior partner kills himself, goes broke,
or leaves his wife for Bob in shipping—all
without resorting to crude buffoonery.

No shaving cream, no cherry bombs or wedgies.
No drunken dancing through the woods at night.
Such revelries pose long-term complications

with group morale and, thus, the bottom line.
No, Fonda's not here. Neither is Anita,
though in a darkened wood alone in autumn,

someone starts to laugh unsupervised
because, wept empty, she can weep no longer.
Is she Anita Dick or Fonda Peters?

She laughs because there's nothing else to do,
because there's worse beneath the worst she feared.
The Humor Institute has work to do.

Jesus Loved His Body

Jesus loved his body, glass
slivers levitating through it
like motes floating up low angles
of sunlight till they slip tenderly
from his skin. For months I brushed
glass from my hair and eased
it through my skin, as if
delivering something new
instead of returning something old
to sunlight. My skin
was a window toward which
I rose. Glass entered me
as I entered it, and Jesus loved his body
as I loved the mountain road
and the pines through which glass
and I together tumbled, rending
each other without intention.
Jesus loved his body. Motes
of window, windshield, frosted
separation float through me, rising,
some of them, but others still descend,
confetti on a parade at the bone,
where out-of-tune drums and trumpets
buzz, saluting Jesus: Jesus,
who loved his body and feared death —
Jesus, who feared everything I fear,
except entering the world.

Self-Portrait as a Family

He's glad his sister visits twice a week,
though twice a week she prays until she faints.
The guards haul her into a plastic chair,

and she wakes chattering about his soul—
first things and last. Her brother, like the guards,
is patient. He winks, but kneels with her, and prays.

At night, lights out, he turns almost reflective
as other inmates serenade the moon
—coyote moans and psychopathic laughter—

and he decides again he's blameless, a victim
of the dictionary. Words so clear to him
mean other things to people who read books.

"I told him if he moved, I'd shoot. He moved.
That's suicide. What else you gonna call it?"
He ponders *his* theology of first

and last—the first of the month, the last of the month.
His story's old, new revenues are falling,
and unsold memoirs jam the family attic.

He has a plan: escape. Kidnap the governor.
Rape him! Or say he did. Back on death row,
with act two of his drama under option,

he can release himself to howls of rapture,
inducing others to seduce the moon.
But first he has a family to support.

Now and Almost Now

Under dawn light,
cars glow, and a paper,
heavy with yesterday,
reposes on the walk.
A boy plodding
toward a bus quickens
to a differential jog.
Already golden,
the soft morning
starts to harden
around a summer
tanager eclipsed
by reddening oaks,
a few leaves
already golden
themselves. The door,
then the storm door,
creak open, the hinges'
high note lower
than the summer tanager's.

The School Bell

If they reach for their coats
or gather books, they will be scolded,
but the children begin, softly,
to buzz. The clock's minute hand
is thirty seconds yet from vertical,
and the fly on the classroom bell
is still and therefore silent, opposite
the little curved iron clapper
tensed, always tensed, over
a bright dimple in the old bell.

Birthday Cake

Eager for good
luck, I sputtered
pink wax
across brown icing
and "Andrew" spelled
in stale letters
peeled from a candy
alphabet.

Among torn
wrapping and small
gifts, I considered:
Six is finished,
seven begun.
Six of what?
Seven of how
many?

     My brothers
ate two of the hard
green letters. Most
of my name, I ate it.

The Mezzanine

Though I was nine,
I should have known
Belk's mezzanine,
that empty noon
between bed linen
and feminine
scents — benign
to girls, strychnine
to me at nine —
was not my Canaan
or Parthenon.
I was a non-
agnostic as I spun in
the aisle, alone,
arms spread, inane,
tame as a nun
but dizzy-drunk, at noon,
that noon, just nine,
on the mezzanine,
alone,
a boy known,
he was sure, to none.

Wigwam Village

The Grand Canyon is just
a big hole in the ground,
my father said, and as we leaned
over the rail, staring
till we were bored and hungry,
he chuckled his destructive chuckle,
by which I learned a hole
can be glorious and still
a hole. Our beds were on a truck
somewhere. Ten and worried,
I hallucinated the highway
strewn with mattresses, shoes,
everything. But as we rolled
out of the desert, I beheld
nineteen huge white teepees,
each with an air conditioner
plastered into the side
and a TV's skeletal wings
spreading over make-believe
lodge poles. I yearned
to sleep in a house tapering
to a single point. In my sleep
I'd float there, looking down
on my dream-paralyzed self

as my family sped past to a home
we already knew we'd leave
in three years, and when we left,
would I long for it, I wondered,
a home I'd not yet seen?

The Imagined Copperhead

The imagined copperhead
hid on the path ahead,
unseen on bronze leaves, unheard,
and a mortal likelihood
at every step. This was childhood,
mine, the woods' jihad
against a boy who'd
intruded among monkshood,
wasp, tick, and nettles haired
with needles. Scrub brush abhorred
him with a horde
of welts, bites, and stings, but he'd
never seen a copperhead,
though he'd looked hard,
taking, as he'd been ordered, heed.
The snake wasn't a falsehood,
though, to him. Dread
was his nature, and he hared
through sunlight and shade, head
swiveling for the copperhead
he'd begun to covet, the ballyhooed
killer a camouflaged godhead
on which his ingrained faith cohered,
and finally his priesthood.

Welder's Smoke

When the light-stunned doe
went stupid, I couldn't fire,
a furtive scruple that meant nothing
to the blue lights that whooped on
behind us, us with two pistols
sliding across the seat. Bobby
slapped the lights off and gunned it,
slamming into the dark. Prey now,
we slewed through switchback
rollercoaster curves and powered down
dust wallows the law didn't know
until, breathless among scraped pine,
sassafras, and kudzu, we watched
blue lights split the dark and the dark
heal three times as the spit in our whispers
dried to welder's smoke — if we were busted,
the acrid taste of our futures.
Around dry mouths, we rolled
the metallic residue of iron, copper,
and zinc fumes, struggling to love it.
The blue lights departed. On moonlit kudzu
we spat, but not bitterly,
the toxic oxides of a harder world,
thinking, once spared the effort,
I could have loved that life.

Suddenly Adult

When I was young, God,
young too, angered
easily and he glared
as I malingered
in innocence, and swaggered
its dancehalls, fingered
an effeminate and beleaguered
mustache, pink snigger
squirming on lips sugared
with purity. God and I tangoed
until we staggered
to a sickened clinch, glued
together with sweat, haggard
and suddenly adult.
                As we've grayed
and grown obliging, each gored
to tact by the other's butterfingered
corrections, we've agreed,
God and I, to safeguard
whatever is left to safeguard
of the other.
                O good
Father Hopkins, a goad
unto this laggard,
and better Herbert, a guide
I dream of following, I am glad,
and so, I think, is God,
to let the Lord's assumption glide.

Two Bourbons Past the Funeral

Two bourbons past the funeral,
we were reading from the thin
old books of the old poet, past old now,
and another old poet fumbled
to his favorite poem. Where was it?
Not this book, but that, and then
he was reading, his voice reverent
and sure, until he caught on a word
like a coat on a barb, and hung there,
a low moan ululating on a long vowel
for the friend he knew almost entirely
from these words and his own voice
reading them. On and on the soft
moaning rose and fell, until he tore free
and snarled, "I told you not to do that."
"Yes, you did," he said, and turned again
to the old poem, reading as if he'd written it,
a small change here, a larger there,
correcting the fictions and false
felicities of youth.

Orpheus in the Garden

In the garden of the Hesperides, where
the golden apples grew, Orpheus caressed
strings that outsang the Sirens, charmed hell,
and softened the heart of Death. The hills crept close
to listen, and marvelous trees, full of dumbstruck birds,
bent toward him.
              The great crowd too bent forward, tense.
Keepers stabbed torches into the starved bear's wounds,
and it stormed the criminal garbed as Orpheus.
The coliseum bawled for justice—or mercy,
if the singer sang as well as legend claimed.

Lord Byron's Boots

From their display case, John Murray VI removed,
his obit said, Lord Byron's boots from time to time, and smeared
hard black wax on dry, two-hundred-year-old leather,
working it into cracks and gouges first burnished
with tallow and lampblack—a job I'd like. *Come now, my man,*
I want to see those elbows fly! If you think I'll wear your work
to promenade the most admired and fashionable whores,
you may go to hell and fuck spiders. And back to work I go
on my own boots, blacking scuffs, and buffing scrapes, gouges,
cuts, and time to an elegant but not excessive luster.

Our Wars

Curled in curled folders, the last reports
were filed by hands infirm now
or gone. Months, even years
go by without our reading
of recovered bones and bits of brass
that shone once on the raked,
immaculate parade grounds of another age.
Our current wars and our current dead
are the headlines. Shelves fill with books
explaining in cool and novel ways
the wars of our youth, but the immense
granite memorials saying "We will never forget"
and "We will always remember" echo
only with the tactful murmuring of caretakers.
The living veterans are too frail to visit,
even the widows are vanishing, and the young
grieve by granite engraved yesterday.

Summer of '09

D.C. / Tehran

No automatic rifle swung up,
assessing me, and I never,
black boots hammering my spine,
humped asphalt helplessly.
For five miles, chanting *Stop the war,*
shouting with other shouters at
a government we almost trusted,
I did not wear black glasses and a mask.
I hung back with some other laughers—
in crowds we always find each other,
laughing at what we all believe.
At home, sunburned, I cracked a beer,
not imagining the latch
shattering, rifle stock
clubbing the skull, military
heel planted on my back. Last month,
I did not, in a Thorazinic monotone, drone
my gratitude to the Brothers,
since purged, at the Intelligence Ministry
for awakening me to my errors.
My father was not summoned
to receive, in bloody, hardening sheets,
my body—each death and forced
confession a scorched tooth
the dragon, in its madness, ripped
from its hot necrotic jaw.

Death Mask of Sargon

Over the sensual, condescending smile of the Great King,
the abyss of his left eye, gouged out, is the left eye of the abyss,
his truest eye. Court sculptors made, broke, melted, cast,
    and recast
copper and tin to flatter the king who "conquered the
    western land
to its farthest point," in victory so "polluted with blood,"
the chronicles tell us, he offended his own god. At his death,
rebels, emerging as artists, speared the true eye
into Sargon's death mask. Two arts: one exquisite artifice,
one rage—and Rage, having gouged the one eye, started on
    the other,
until, in the greatness of his artistry, he stopped.

Stalin's Laughter

At the secret policeman's feast, Pauker sagged, drunk,
between two officers, as he aped Zinoviev, hiccupping hilariously
and staggering over watery, risible feet as he was dragged
to the firing post. A devotee of Momus, son of Night, Stalin was,
and Pauker, knowing it, mouthed words
he could not, in feigned panic, propel from his tongue
because dysphonia is always funny, the ratchet and catch
of fractious breath farcical. Pauker fell prostrate, as Zinoviev
    had fallen,
and he clutched the boots of his mock guards
and cried, *Please, for God's sake, comrade! Call*
Yosip Vissarionovich. And Stalin, evoked as savior, roared,
basso buffo. Pauker pushed harder, as a jester must, raising
    his arms
to the banquet hall's beamed ceiling, as Zinoviev had raised his
to the fuliginous brown clouds crowded over the prison yard,
and cried, "Hear, O Israel, our God is the only God." Stalin
choked on ungovernable mirth. Tears rolled
almost onto the mustache whose likeness, metaphorical,
to *Blattella germanica,* the German cockroach, paid Mandelstam's
ambagious passage to a common grave outside
a transit camp. Stalin slashed his thick hand—Enough!
    Enough!—
commanding mercy upon the festive executioners laughing
    helplessly.

The Return of the Magi

Deep-sea cameras beam
green-on-green grainy
flickers: The magi, cradling
enameled caskets,
rock woodenly over horses
mincing up the vertiginous
tilt of an obsidian trench.
They do not speak. They merely
flow with the glacial undulations
of gilt-harnessed geldings and
the mercurial surge
of underwater current, their features
eroding like the harbor stones
of sunken Alexandria,
blurred but eternal.
From long immersion, they've turned
to verdigris: purple robes
now verdigris, verdigris
their geldings, their hands and faces
verdigris as they ascend
from black to black-green water,
returning with the same apocalyptic
languor at which they left.

4

Villanelle with a Refrain from the *Wall Street Journal*

Your twenties, thirties, forties, you're a bull—
if you think of life as something like the Dow.
Though death, of course, is unavoidable,

you're rising so fast rising's almost dull,
your daily highs untested by a low.
Your twenties, thirties, forties, you're a bull,

and life, for now, is fast and overfull—
for now, you might say, chuckling, *for now*—
though death, of course, is unavoidable.

You're savvy enough, I'm sure, and fully able
to plan for when the market starts to slow.
Your twenties, thirties, forties, you're a bull,

and all your hours, all, are billable,
as you tell others what, but mostly how,
though death, of course, is unavoidable.

Like contracts, life is fully voidable,
allow deferring soon to *disallow.*
Your twenties, thirties, forties, you're a bull,
though death, of course, is unavoidable.

Night Harvest

From my neighbor's dark garden I harvested asparagus;
I pilfered slender spears from their feathery bed
and clipped buds of American Beauty. All spring
and into early autumn I savored a fragrance
redolent of theft. Through summer I plucked squash,
beans, and more squash from his vines.
In the yard where I watched his daughter marry,
I divided hostas by moonlight and daylilies too,
keeping half. My neighbor's dead, the house for sale,
and after dark his garden's mine to love and plunder.

In a Distant Room

I hurled lime beneath the house
and through the attic. I scrubbed
the baseboards too, with bleach,
the way I'd washed them as a boy
each time we moved, and washed
again if I had done it poorly
to Mother's wrinkled nose.
Do you smell it? I asked everyone.
Yeah, sort of. No, not really.
Unseen robins thump the windows,
woodpeckers pound the clapboards,
vanishing as I open the door,
and one insistent cricket
clicks beneath my bed
till dawn, invisible in the dark.
In the paper I read of singed
bees swarming from a flue
and a yellow stain spreading
down someone's wall, the house
humming with multitudinous wings,
the plaster hot with honey
where the honey bomb pulsed.
Then at a margin of the mind,
in a room where she was smoking,

drinking coffee, and worrying
about worry—all the things,
the many things that must
and will go wrong—my dead mother,
as she often does, died again.

Broadcasting Winter Rye

In even, overlapping arcs,
seed flew from his fingertips
and rained across the field,
not for harvest, but to sprout
and be plowed under,
so his truck—corn, mostly—
could flourish on rot
and nitrogen. Quick
rivulets of sweat
sluiced down his flushed
tight face as I approached him,
flinging rye across
last spring's damp furrows.
We met midfield,
our buckets empty. He swayed,
I held his shoulder, and after
three or four harsh breaths,
he lifted my hand away. Brown
seed stuck to his sweat-
drenched face. Dead man,
dead man, dead man
my uncle was, when the green
rye cracked the frosted dirt
and no one turned it under.

Bess

Fern fronds, gracefully placed,
curved over the open casket,
and in the sturdy, sweeping breeze
of air conditioning, they swayed,
waved, beckoned, and my aunt's
hands moved, or seemed to,
or I willed it so. Silver hair,
silver dress, silver face,
silver coffin. From the florist's
where she worked: perfect ferns,
not a bent frond or broken rachis,
not a single brown-tipped pinna.
Close, though, I saw one glossy
green leaflet had fallen on her thin
silver hands—on it, a double row
of black-brown spores, perfect
near-circles perfectly spaced,
no sorus touching another,
the way we buried her, halfway
between her husband and her son.

March

As at death's threshold
we shiver, made old
without growing old,
by the March cold.
But under the snow-
flakes' slow
tumbling adagio—
by winter's low
sun, lit gold—
we almost unfold
our hearts to cold,
almost loosen our hold
on what we know
of blown snow
shadowing the window
and the lamp's dull glow
like a debt we owe
to Plato, but for now
withhold. It's cold,
but no longer zero.
Warm enough to snow.
We are almost consoled.

The Funeral Sermon

Almost droll
in its assault on *magisterial*,
my father's funeral
sermon made me prowl,
—agitated—from bean casserole
to escarole
salad, then taco casserole,
and back all afternoon, in thrall
to Dad's every growl,
cramped certitude, and corporal
wavering lost to shrill
sacral
cant. The pastoral
story was Dad's own, though, frail
as it is: Faith and God steamroll
death. His wife's and daughter's role
was to die—a trial
of faith, not cruel
so much as natural,
when the supernatural
is, as it was for him, literal.
His cloistral
withdrawal, according to the minister's drawl,
was grace, and his temporal
forfeitures fat collateral
on eternity. It felt surreal
(can there be a funeral

without, now, the word *surreal?*)
to hear Dad's stoic control
and loneliness spiral
heavenward on genial praise, real
enough for the general,
one supposes. An orchestral
hymn flared through the stereo's cloth grille.
Cold waves over the deep water roll,
we sang, some voices shrill,
mine guttural,
my brother's slow as a crawl—
our voices one and several,
a visceral,
not unmagisterial,
chorale.

Harvest

Sometimes I'm eager for the autumn wind's
cold edge to slice
brown leaves from black limbs
and harry them, blade at their backs,
down damp asphalt — and eager too
for a muscular wind to shove pale sky
through four days' changes
in an afternoon, a long gray wind
that drives me east
before it, afraid and happy, a blown radio
garbling the songs of my youth, the songs
themselves one
with the greater wind, the gray
scythe slicing trees and stripped fields,
carving summer free of our callused hold,
while the moon dangles huge
above the highway's dazzling interchanges,
and I pretend it is my destination
as I wish I imagined the knife edge at my back,
and I am the wind
until it takes me.
Cold? I'm already cold.

Having Labored All Night

Having labored all night
and awakened empty, your courage
exhausted, your losses epic,
and your desires beyond anything
waking has ever required,
your self narrows now
to one substance, flesh,
and that substance consigned
to an obligation vital
to everyone you love
and to history, the whole of it,
though how you cannot say
because you're gratefully
forgetting everything you've done,
though your teeth still ache
from exertion, the sacrifices
borne all night, and the valor
expended, as you resolve
into sunlit blurred determinations.

Grand Expensive Vista

As we sipped and mingled,
regaled
with oldfangled
canapés and beguiled,
or entertained at least, by gargled
oldies, I disengaged
and angled
across grass tenderly groomed,
past where electric tiki torches gleamed,
and, alone, gazed,
now truly beguiled,
at my hosts' grand
expensive vista, mortgaged,
yes, and yes, remortgaged.
A low gold
moon glowed
against a plush black sky gauzed,
even filigreed,
with stars. Gowned
in old-growth oaks glazed
with moonlight over their autumn gilt,
the hills glowed
in concord with the golden moon. I lingered,
glad—discomfited and glad—
at what my friends' greed
for beauty afforded me. I argued,
self against self, what they'd gained

and lost, and me with them, entangled
as friendship entangles. I nearly groaned
aloud with want before my friend grabbed
my elbow. "Gorgeous, eh?" I grinned
and agreed,
my voice greased
with hidden envy. From behind us, grilled
sirloin, pedigreed
meat sublimating on embers, triggered
another hunger. Life was not just good,
but too good:
aged beef, aged wine after bourbon. We hungered,
and all the way back to his engorged
glass table, hunger was our guide.

Bryce Hospital: The Old Cemetery

Down the parched hill,
crosses, like rows
of cast-iron clovers,
sagged. The bodies
beneath them slipped,
slid, and gathered
into a huge composite
skeleton, I thought,
as I sat among
the graves of the once
insane. They can't
stay separate;
no one does, not even
the evening travelers
speeding home
to different houses.

Between the traffic
racing west
into the sun, that
symbol of endings,
and the Black Warrior
River dawdling
toward the Gulf, that
figure of oblivion,
it was madness
I feared. Insanity's

plea for purity
and pleasing, anxious
certitude still
whispers for the self
to abandon itself,
though in sunlight, I've
relinquished most
such luxuries.
Out of respect,
I visit here my yet
potential forefathers,
their names, their years
lost to numbered
crosses sliding
down the parched hill.

Over the river
I heard the erratic
bang, bang,
of distant hammers.
Building or destroying?
In a graveyard — bang! —
everything is a symbol.
The blows were slow
— measure, cut,
raise, level —
none of which I saw —

and bang, bang,
bang: nails
were gunned flush.
It was creation, not
destruction's indisputable
quick ecstasies,
and I took hammering
for a curfew bell
and walked home.

Fleeing Time

Swinging a block
of frozen chicken
thighs in a plastic
sack—that's
what I think of when
I think of my twenties,
quick-stepping home
under broken lights
to the graffitied
complex my fucked
jobs forced me to.
The frozen meat
was a weapon. I swung it
like a blackjack
and banged the stop sign
like a gong. With it,
I hammered flat
my mailbox door, curled
by a crowbar. I hammered,
hammered, hammered.
No door opened,
no one yelled,
tempus fucking
fugited,
and one day I opened
an umbrella and saw
inside it the large

brick house I'd own,
a house owned
by other owners,
a wife who'd been
someone else's wife,
as I had been
someone's husband,
and I was smiling a smile
smiled by many
happy people.

Tempus, Tempus,
linger yet awhile.

Beyond My Footfall

A footfall on the fallen leaves,
my footfall,
careful—I am careful
not to trouble
mushrooms furled
in the spongy, crumbling duff
or scuffle
the softening mast muffling
my steps. All night small fowl,
pierced by spring,
squabble toward triumphal
arias. High-blooded
harmonies fill
a canopy full
already with the almost metallic
odor of chlorophyll,
the blue air perfumed green. Feel
life lift from each leaf
lightly. Call it joyful.
Call it plentiful or prayerful.
Call it summer's fuel
that in the darkening fall
blazes firelessly, xanthophyll
like gold and copper foil
coruscant beyond my footfall,
metaphor, and last belief,
to the next unfailing
regeneration faithful.

Acknowledgments

I am grateful to the editors of the following journals, in which some of these poems first appeared:

Academy of American Poets, Poem-a-Day series (at Poets.org): "Steppingstone." *AGNI:* "Bess." *Atlantic Monthly:* "Under the Maypole," "In the Arboretum," "Night Harvest," "Villanelle with a Refrain from the *Wall Street Journal.*" *Court Green:* "Broadcasting Winter Rye." *Georgia Review:* "A Mystery." *Gettysburg Review:* "In Arcadia, the Home of Pan," "Suddenly Adult." *Hopkins Review:* "Birth of a Naturalist," "Now and Almost Now," "Self-Portrait as a Family." *Image:* "The Offices," "Orpheus in the Garden." *Kenyon Review:* "Death Mask of Sargon," "Lord Byron's Boots," "Stalin's Laughter." *Literary Imagination:* "Foresworn," "A Joke Is Washed Up on a Desert Island," "Princess after Princess." *New Republic:* "Welder's Smoke." *Paris Review:* "The Wild Swans Skip Coole." *Poetry:* "Grand Expensive Vista," "Swordfish," "The Funeral Sermon," "The Imagined Copperhead." *River Styx:* "Wigwam Village." *Salmagundi:* "Jesus Loved His Body." *Sewanee Review:* "Fairy Tale with Ex-Wife," "March." *Shenandoah:* "The Humor Institute." *Slate:* "Summer of '09." *Southern Quarterly:* "Mattress under Sumac." *Southern Review:* "In a Distant Room," "The Mezzanine," "The Return of the Magi." *Southwest Review:* "At Evening, Eden." *Virginia Quarterly Review:* "Autumn's Author," "Our Wars."

I'm very grateful to my editor Michael Collier, whose encouragement, care, and astute critical eye made this book better. Christianne Balk and Adam Vines gave me the great gifts of close readings at a crucial time, and my agent, Marianne Merola, was her usual helpful self. Thank you all.